FINDING GOD
IN ORDINARY TIME

Christine Marie Eberle

FINDING GOD
IN ORDINARY TIME

Daily Meditations

CHRISTINE MARIE EBERLE

GREEN PLACE BOOKS | *Brattleboro, Vermont*

Printed in the United States

10 9 8 7 6 5 4 3 2 1

GREEN WRITERS PRESS is a Vermont-based publisher whose mission is to spread a message of hope and renewal through the words and images we publish. Throughout we will adhere to our commitment to preserving and protecting the natural resources of the earth. To that end, a percentage of our proceeds will be donated to environmental activist groups and the author's charity of choice, My Place Germantown (myplacegermantown.org). Green Writers Press gratefully acknowledges support from individual donors, friends, and readers to help support the environment and our publishing initiative. GREEN PLACE BOOKS curates books that tell literary and compelling stories with a focus on writing about place.

GREEN
PLACE
BOOKS

Giving Voice to Writers & Artists Who Will Make the World a Better Place
Green Writers Press | Brattleboro, Vermont | www.greenwriterspress.com

"Praying" from the volume *Thirst* by Mary Oliver, published by Beacon Press, Boston. Copyright © 2006 by Mary Oliver. Used herewith by permission of the Charlotte Sheedy Literary Agency, Inc.

ISBN: 978-1-7320815-3-6

COVER DESIGN BY ASHA HOSSAIN

Women's Business Enterprise
National Council
WBENC

PRINTED ON PAPER WITH PULP THAT COMES FROM FSC-CERTIFIED FORESTS, MANAGED FORESTS THAT GUARANTEE RESPONSIBLE ENVIRONMENTAL, SOCIAL, AND ECONOMIC PRACTICES BY McNAUGHTON & GUNN, A WOMAN-OWNED BUSINESS CERTIFIED BY THE WOMEN'S BUSINESS ENTERPRISE NATIONAL COUNCIL.

Contents

PART TWO: MESSENGERS OF GRACE / 29

PART THREE: FAR FROM HOME / 55

PART FOUR: WORKING IT OUT / 81

Nothing is more practical than finding God,

that is, than falling in love

in a quite absolute, final way.

What you are in love with,

what seizes your imagination,

will affect everything.

It will decide what will get you out of bed in the morning,

what you will do with your evenings,

how you will spend your weekends,

what you read,

who you know,

what breaks your heart,

and what amazes you with joy and gratitude.

Fall in love,

stay in love

and it will decide everything.

—PEDRO ARUPE, SJ

Origins and Observations

"I'm really glad I'm always able to pray so well," said no one, ever.

In my quarter-century of spiritual conversations with young and not-so-young adults, one theme has come up over and over again: people of faith are anxious about prayer. We know we should pray, and often we try, but we don't think we're very good at it, and we're sure other people are better. We yearn to feel close to God, but most days, we just feel clueless.

It doesn't help that some people reach adulthood with way too much religious baggage—images of God that are problematic yet persistent—while others arrive with suitcases nearly empty, having gotten through adolescence without acquiring a scrap of religious vocabulary. Whether we start by struggling to erase the picture of God as an angry old white guy with a beard, or by staring at an alarmingly blank piece of paper, moving into a mature relationship with the living God is both a challenge and the work of a lifetime.

The people of Jesus' day were not so different. If they were, he wouldn't have had to resort to so many similes. Just think of all the things Jesus said the reign of God was *like:* an old woman; a new wineskin; a merchant's search for fine pearls; a mustard seed. Urgently he piled simile upon metaphor upon analogy—anything that could reveal the ways of God in the language of ordinary experience.

I did not always understand this. The particular flavor of my Roman Catholic upbringing didn't dwell on experience and metaphor; it emphasized answers and rules. In matters of faith, it was important to know the right answers and abide by the rules. And so I did. I was a good daughter, a good student, a good Catholic (or so I thought)… and unbearably self-righteous.

It wasn't until the fifteenth year of my Catholic education that I realized there was more to faith than doctrinal certainty. At Saint Joseph's, Philadelphia's Jesuit university, I majored in English but was drawn to campus ministry for reasons having less to do with the appeal of religion than with the appealing guy at a retreat sign-up table. In college, I discovered that faith could also include things like service, community, and social justice. I figured out that Mass could actually be a joyful and voluntary activity that fed the spirit, not just an obligation to be gotten out of the way each weekend. And I discovered that prayer—which to that point I had only experienced as unidirectional activities like asking, thanking, and apologizing—could actually be an encounter with God. So I picked up theology as a double major, went on for a master's degree in pastoral ministry at Boston College (another fine Jesuit institution), served in a soup kitchen and as a hospital chaplain, and—fast forward—have spent twenty-five years working as a college campus minister.

I will always be grateful for my Jesuit education. Some 1,500 years after Jesus used all those similes to get through to ordinary people, Saint Ignatius of Loyola, the founder of the Jesuit order of priests, urged his followers to "find God in all things," a concept that has seized imaginations ever since. Every experience has the ability to teach us something of God, Ignatius believed, if only we pay attention.

That's what this little book is about: paying attention. God longs to communicate with us, and uses whatever material is available. If we can train our vision to notice, open our hearts to listen, and allow our spirits to savor something each day, then our prayer can be transformed into a long, loving conversation. Some days, it will be an argument; at other times, God will just crack us up. We may be humbled, challenged, affirmed, or consoled, but we will never be bored.

And so I give you *Finding God in Ordinary Time.* It's a bit of a play on words. In my Roman Catholic tradition, Ordinary Time is the long liturgical season that offers a little teaser between Christmas and Lent, and then stretches out for almost half a year between Pentecost and Advent. Many prayer resources are designed for those special seasons, so I'm happy to provide something for this less dramatic, more ordered procession of weeks. For people of any or no faith tradition, however, "ordinary time" also refers to the way we experience our days. Each life contains certain moments of awe. We welcome a baby into the world, or accompany a loved one out of it. We go on retreat and have a profound religious experience. We take the vacation of a lifetime and sink to the ground in reverence at the edge of the Grand Canyon or beneath a bright field of stars. These experiences are real, but they're also rare. Literally as well as liturgically, most of our days are spent in ordinary time.

The chapters of this book are organized into four different "terrains" where I have experienced the presence of God—sometimes at once, but usually upon prayerful reflection.

- The first is a place where most agree it is easy to spot the hand of the Creator: in the natural world, whenever we are awake to see it.
- The second is more challenging: in the delightful and difficult people around us— messengers of grace for those with ears to hear.

- The third lies beyond our comfort zone, in the shifting perspective gained when we experience another culture far from home.
- And the fourth is in the everyday struggle of working it out: grappling with our flaws, wrestling with our identity, making hard decisions—the real nitty-gritty of everyday life in ordinary time.

Because liturgical Ordinary Time is structured in weeks—and because I really like structure—each terrain contains seven chapters in the form of daily meditations. Every day begins with a true story that segues into a bit of musing on lessons learned, and then poses a question or two for your own pondering. There's also a short Scripture quote connected to the theme, there to ground your reflection and give you something to hold onto through the day.

There is a progression here, but there is also fluidity. It doesn't matter whether you proceed through this book in an orderly fashion, or simply pray with whatever phrase or image strikes you. There is no right way to do this. There are no rules. There is only you, a person in relationship with God. Do whatever nourishes the friendship; that's what it means to pray.

May each of your ordinary days be extraordinarily blessed.

— *Christine*

PART ONE

AWAKE TO SEE

The heavens declare the glory of God, Psalm 19 proclaims. If you have ever seen the stars on a clear night beyond the reach of light pollution, you know what this means.

I will never forget the first time I went camping. Grumbling my way out of the tent for a 3 A.M. call of nature (pun intended), I was stunned into silence by the beauty that awaited me just outside the canvas flap. Had the earth relocated? Surely, the stars had never been this bright, or this close, or this many? If I were interviewing God for the job of Creator and said, "Can I see a sample of your work?" this would have been the ideal thing to pull from the divine portfolio.

When the Bible is confusing, the denominational voices conflicting, or the inner wisdom fleeting, just go outside. Want to know how God feels about diversity? Look at a field of wildflowers. Wonder if God has a sense of humor? Consider the pelican. Not really sure you get this whole resurrection business? Notice the determined shoots of the first flowers of spring, pushing through the frozen ground of winter's last stand.

With God's fingerprints all over it, nature is an endless source of spiritual insight.

CHAPTER 1

Finding God in the Morning Sky

From the rising of the sun to its setting, let the name of the LORD be praised.
—PSALM 113:3

I LOVE A COMPLICATED SUNRISE. Whether I'm on retreat by myself or at the beach with my family, I always want to watch the sun come up. If I oversleep (which my relatives call "getting up at a normal time for a person on vacation"), I arise well rested but vaguely disappointed. *How was the sunrise this morning? What did I miss?*

When I join my extended family each August for a week at the Jersey shore, mornings find me on my uncle's deck with coffee in hand, watching the sun come up over the ocean. With the exception of rainy days, every sunrise is unique and glorious, but the complicated ones are the best.

On a perfectly clear day, the sun will simply appear; but on a cloudy morning, I can discern its progress only by the effect it has on the world around it. The drama begins long before the sun reaches the horizon. Low-hanging clouds lit from below begin to glow. As the sun progresses upward, the colors are straight out of a thesaurus: not just pink, purple, and orange, but crimson, scarlet, violet, amethyst, and vermillion. A tiny break appears in the clouds and the sun dazzles through, making the sea sparkle, and the ocean changes hue as if touched by a magic wand. The sun disappears just as quickly, lighting the tops of the lower clouds as it ascends. Then the whole beach brightens and the fog begins to lift, revealing the big rollercoaster on the boardwalk three miles away. Seagulls exult; sometimes dolphins break the surface as if they don't want to miss the show, either.

Morning has arrived. I am grateful each time I am awake to see it.

I love a complicated sunrise for the same reason I love my job in college campus ministry. Just as the sun is rendered more beautiful by its effect on the clouds, God's glory shines most clearly when it touches the shadowed parts of people's lives.

A timid student begins to glow in the warmth of a faith community. Foggy lack of direction gives way to the illuminated path of a discovered call. God's healing power touches broken places—disappointments, abuses, failures, betrayals—and renders hearts stronger than they were before. People in pain discover that the darkness in their lives does not have to stay dark, and when God's light reaches those troubled crevices, they are transformed from sources of shame into radiant signs of the divine. Morning arrives in its own way for each one, as clouds give way to light.

I am grateful each time I am awake to see it.

The next time you are able to pray during sunrise, let images of your own life's transformations wash over you. Can you perceive how God may have been at work in you, even in your darkest times?

CHAPTER 2

Finding God in Plain Sight

Do you have eyes and not see?
—MARK 8:18

I DON'T FLY WEST WELL. The time change invariably undoes me. Until my body adjusts, I keep waking up on east coast time, no matter when I've gone to bed or how early it happens to be in California. Before I learned to travel with a jar of emergency coffee (instant, so you know it's an emergency), I always spent my first mornings on the left coast as that crazy lady hovering on the sidewalk, waiting for the café to open.

Many years ago, in San Diego for a meeting, I decided to embrace my insomnia and drive up the coast to La Jolla. I hopped in the rental car, timed my arrival for the moment the first coffee shop would unlock its doors, then took my steaming brew to a bench with a good view of the harbor and its rocky beach. There were sea lions there, I'd been told. Perhaps I'd catch a glimpse of one.

It certainly was pretty, and the weather was nicer than at home, but I really didn't see what all the fuss was about. I scanned for sea lions. Nothing. (Maybe they weren't morning people.) I finished my coffee, but it was still too soon to return to the campus where I was staying, so I pulled a book from my backpack and tried to read. I was distracted, though. *What was that noise?* I looked up, wondering if perhaps a sea lion were arriving at last. No such luck. The rocks were moving, though.

The rocks were moving?

In one spectacular moment of refocusing, I realized there were no rocks on the beach, only sea lions—probably a hundred of them. As the sun rose, they were stretching, jostling for a better position, waddling to higher ground, grunting and barking as they went. Now that I saw them, I couldn't un-see them—or imagine how I'd missed them in the first place.

What else am I overlooking? That's the question that begs to be asked. If I can miss a hundred giant mammals right in front of me because I don't expect to see them there, what else am I failing to notice?

I think the answer lies in the question of expectation. Too often, we only see what we're predisposed to find. In movies, for example, it's a common plot device for someone to pass unnoticed by donning the uniform of a waitress, postal worker, or security guard—someone we see every day, but don't really observe.

Overlooking a colony of sea lions is embarrassing, but I can live with that. What I don't want to miss is the *people* God has placed right in front of me. Each one has a name and a story. Each has a past and a dreamed-of future. Each is carrying something difficult. Each has wisdom to share. What would it cost me to make eye contact and find out?

Is there someone you see every day, but rarely notice? Try shifting your focus today. Say hello. Ask a question. Discover another of God's beloveds, hidden in plain sight.

CHAPTER 3

Finding God in the Backyard

Teach us to count our days aright, that we may gain wisdom of heart.
—PSALM 90:12

IBOUGHT MY HOUSE IN THE MIDDLE OF WINTER. It's a small row home with a fenced-in backyard just big enough for all the fruits, flowers, vegetables, and herbs I can reasonably tend. The realtor's photos had included a nice shot of colorful perennials out front, but the back remained a mystery until spring.

Once the weather warmed, each month brought surprises. There were giant yellow tulips, a strawberry patch, orange lilies, Shasta daisies, chocolate and white irises, and burgundy chrysanthemums. But the most delightful surprise, that first summer, was the wild morning glories. They crept up the back fence from the outside and tumbled over it, purple and blue trumpets reaching for the sky with dramatic abandon.

I watched in wonder, as they grew more lush and plentiful. They covered the spent strawberry patch and kept on blooming, gloriously.

Then they took down my gladiolas.

One morning, just as the glads were beginning to open, I looked out my kitchen window and they were *gone*—strangled and pulled to the ground by morning glory vines like flowers in an episode of *Law and Order: Garden Unit.* Going outside for a closer look, I noticed incipient vines springing up in the grass, at the edge of the tomato patch, and around the sugar snap peas. An internet search revealed the plant's common name: *bindweed.* Quickly, my love affair with morning glories ended, and my fight to regain control of the garden began.

Since that first summer, I have learned to spot the pesky plants early, and to pluck them mercilessly. It requires vigilance, diligence, and persistence. I need to pay attention—to look at the garden each day with a careful eye and see what's really going on. It's like having a spiritual tutorial in my own backyard.

According to an old proverb, "the good is often the enemy of the best." My plot is tiny, and while morning glories are not evil, they don't understand moderation. I can't sustain the plants I most desire in their presence.

How to create space for the things we really value is a perennial question. Each day, we make choices about our time and attention. Ironically, the people and passions we cherish most require careful tending, while mindless pastimes tend to run amok effortlessly. Inevitably, a choice for one is a choice *against* another.

There will always be plenty of worthy things to compete for our attention. The least we can do is uproot the less worthy ones.

In a spirit of prayer, make a list of the people and pursuits in your life that are most important to you. Are you giving them the attention they deserve? What takes over your time like a creeping vine? Is there one change God might suggest?

CHAPTER 4

Finding God in the Compost Bin

Happy the one who finds wisdom, the one who gains understanding!
—PROVERBS 3:13

I WOULD CALL IT A MIRACLE if I didn't understand the science. Eggshells, carrot peels, grapefruit rinds, and coffee grounds in; fertile dirt out! For the past eight years, all my kitchen scraps—and a fair bit of my shredded leaves—have gone into that wondrous box, yet it has never overflowed.

One of my favorite days each year comes in early spring, when I slide open the bottom panel, pull out a shovelful of rich compost, and start digging it into my garden beds. There, it will fertilize the tender beginnings of lettuce, arugula, hot peppers, and sweet potatoes—bits of which will find their way back into the top of the bin as summer progresses. It's like a backyard Rumpelstiltskin, spinning garbage into gold.

The only thing that ever disappointed me there was a bag of whole-grain snack chips I had purchased (impulsively) on the strength of an advertisement that *the bag itself* was compostable. I devoured the chips, dutifully cut up the bag into little pieces, and tossed them into the top of the bin. Two years later, I inserted my shovel into the bottom and pulled out beautiful, rich dirt—and tiny bits of shiny chip bag. Despite the marketing, this trash had not, in fact, become treasure.

The compost bin is such a rich metaphor for the spiritual life. The seemingly useless things of our past—the failures, disappointments, and tragedies—can be transformed over time into something incredibly useful for nurturing fledgling growth (our own, and that of others). But we have to be willing to do the interior work.

We would never throw our raw kitchen scraps directly onto the garden and expect them to do anything but attract vermin. The same is true of our unprocessed experiences; they are useless in their present state. We have to subject them to the heat of reflection, the rainwater of tears, and the fresh air of conversation with the guide of our choice, whether a spiritual director, counselor, or insightful friend. That's what breaks down our wretchedness and softens it into wisdom.

And of course, as with my failed experiment, there is no shortcut to spiritual growth. All those self-help schemes (spiritual, psychological, or physical) that promise results without effort are almost certainly gimmicks that will ultimately disappoint. They are the shiny chip bags of the inner life.

The desires they stir in us are worth paying attention to, because the goals they advertise are laudable. We just need to figure out how to pursue them sustainably—embracing not only the results we want, but also the hard work needed to get there.

Is there a raw experience in your past that has been transformed into wisdom? Can you identify the process it went through? What needs more time in your spiritual compost bin now?

Chapter 5

Finding God in Stillness

Be still and know that I am God!
—Psalm 46:11

MY FAVORITE LOCAL SPOT TO WALK is a five-mile loop through Ridley Creek State Park. The place has it all: challenging hills and flat expanses; shade and sun; cornfields and colonial ruins. There's even a picnic area with restrooms. One summer, I filled in a gap from my childhood reading by listening to *The Chronicles of Narnia* in its entirety on the Ridley loop, and for my forty-ninth birthday, I hoofed it with my brother's dog.

In addition to the countless times I've done the loop alone, I've often taken friends, and I can still recall some of the conversations that unfolded, going deeper into our topics as we went deeper into the woods. There have been moments of great hilarity, like the family outing during which we discovered how many adults it takes to push a fully occupied double stroller up a steep incline. (Three!) Whether alone or in company, the best part of the walk is the mile that runs along the creek. And the best part of *that* is the chance to spot the heron.

Of course, it's probably not the same heron; I've been doing this walk for considerably longer than one bird's lifespan, and it's not like I can tell them apart. But year after year, there is a particular bend in the creek where, if you slow down, look carefully, and get lucky, there she is. And if you have exceptional patience and expendable time, the real fun begins: waiting for her to move.

The heron stands motionless, gaze fixed on the shallow water around her. Occasionally, she will take one excruciatingly slow stride to better position herself. When the heedless prey has wandered close enough, she moves with lightning speed, stabbing her beak into the water to grab her next meal—or one for her offspring. Only then does she spread her magnificent wings and soar back to the treetops.

My favorite description of contemplation (which I am probably paraphrasing because I've never been able to find the reference) is this: *Stay until you see something you might have missed.* If the heron were advising us, she might add, *"Stay still."* Just as splashing about in the creek will only drive the fish away, our restless bodies and careening thoughts make it difficult to settle down in prayer.

I know the heron's advice may sound unappealing at first. When we hear "stay still," we might remember being hushed by our parents, commanded into boring motionlessness so we wouldn't bother anybody. Who wants *that* as an adult? But immobility is not contemplation; it's just self-control. To be still in prayer is to trust that God has something to say, something to show, something that will only come after we quiet our turbulent mind.

This is where the heron becomes our teacher. We have to be *hungry* for the things that only come to us in stillness.

Do you have trouble being still? Try finding a place in nature where you can sit with all your senses engaged. What do you notice? What comes to you?

CHAPTER 6

Finding God at the Campsite

Let me dwell in your tent forever, take refuge in the shelter of your wings.
—PSALM 61:5

I WAS NOT RAISED OUTDOORSY. My family didn't picnic. We didn't barbecue. In my whole life, I don't think I ever saw my mother cook a piece of meat outside. Taking a plate of cold cuts to the screened-in porch was as close as we got to dining alfresco. And since my parents wouldn't even stay at a B&B because it would be too much rubbing-of-elbows with strangers, it goes without saying that we did not *camp*.

Then, in my forties, I fell in love with a Boy Scout dad and converted to camping like a sinner at an altar call. Now I can't wait to pack up the tent (and the air mattress; allowances must be made for middle-aged backs) and head to our favorite campground on the Delaware shore.

At Cape Henlopen, it's not the train or fire station whistle that awakens me, but birds chirping and neighbors quietly unzipping their tent flaps. No coffee timer has my morning cup ready to go; instead, I fill the pot, light the camp stove, and settle in for the percolating. I smell the pine needles under my feet, the salty breeze off the ocean, and the intriguing aroma of someone's breakfast cooking nearby. Once our coffee is good and dark, I pour it into my travel mug and take a slow walkabout, watching the morning fog dissipate as the sun warms the trees. I shed my sweatshirt. Porter makes breakfast. We chat, read, and watch the world go by. I gather the dishes to wash at the water pump. We pack a lunch, secure our groceries from the squirrels, and bike to the beach, or to town. In late afternoon, we return and shower, maybe stretch out in the golden sunshine while it lasts. Then it's time to begin the languorous process of lighting a fire, grilling something delicious, and passing the evening hours between firelight and starlight. Sleep. Repeat.

I love camping because it brings me into contact with spiritual realities from which modern conveniences ordinarily insulate me. Things happen in real time at the campsite. The fire takes as long as it takes to boil water; the sun takes as long as it takes to dry towels. The weather is what it is; we may accommodate, but we can't avoid it. We gaze at glowing sunsets instead of glowing computer screens. We behold nature. We behold one another. We come into what Wendell Berry, in his poem of the same name, calls "the peace of wild things." There are very few opportunities for multitasking.

Why is it easier to feel close to God in the woods? Is it simply the presence of so much creation? I think it's also the absence of so much distraction. In "regular" life, the demands of the day and the omnipresence of technology distance us from God, from one another, and from our deepest selves.

Fortunately, we don't have to erect a tent to silence the chatter. We just have to be intentional about wanting that peace more than we want the alternative.

Where can you go to connect with spiritual realities and disconnect from the chatter, even briefly? How soon can you get there? What's stopping you?

CHAPTER 7

Finding God After the Storm

At dusk weeping comes for the night; but at dawn there is rejoicing.
—PSALM 30:6

THE HEAVENS OPENED just as we were about to leave for our monthly faith-sharing group at Jack's house. It had been one of those oppressively hot summer days when the humidity is practically visible, and the evening storm a given. The rain fell in torrents. Gutters overflowed almost at once, rivers ran down every street, and the wind whipped violently through the trees. The siren at the volunteer fire station began to wail. If ever there were a night to stay on the couch, this was it; but we ran through the downpour to the car, dove in, and began the treacherous drive.

We were only halfway there when the sun broke through the storm. Though it was still teeming, the clouds began to blow away and sun came streaming right through the rain, transfiguring the familiar roads with a celestial sparkle. Every leafy tree glistened with raindrops. Pine needles, knocked from their branches, released an intoxicating fragrance. Steam from the wet pavement glowed in the sudden sunlight. What had been a frightening trip only minutes ago now seemed like a journey through fairyland. Held in that rare moment of storm and sun together, we experienced a beauty both breathtaking and fleeting. *What does this remind me of?* I wondered. And suddenly, I knew: the moments of sweet joy that can spring up in the midst of profound sorrow.

The hours before and after my mother's death shone like this. Mom was only sixty-seven, and had been diagnosed with cancer just ten weeks earlier; she had sickened with the violence of a summer storm. Yet those last awful hours gave me precious memories. Leaving the hospital where my brother and I were about to keep an all-night vigil, our cousin Gene realized we might be hungry, and did a pizza-and-milkshake run before starting his long drive home. Knowing me well, our cousin Susan went to my apartment to make sure the cat had enough food, then thought to go looking for my extra migraine medicine, just in case. My colleague John showed up at my parents' house the next day with the biggest tray of sandwiches I'd ever seen, with which we fed the multitudes all week long.

These acts sound too simple to matter this much to me, but each memory warms my heart still. In my recollection of those tear-washed days, they sparkle with a goodness that can only come from God. When we are too shut down to pray, surely God communicates through ordinary and extraordinary kindnesses. From loved ones or strangers, thoughtful acts at terrible times shine with tender care. Such poignant memories are tokens of love from the One who weeps with us—and for us—in the midst of the storm.

Allow yourself to drift back in memory to a painful time in your life. Where were the incidents of unexpected kindness or moments of grace? Imagine them as gifts from your loving God. Try to linger with whatever feelings arise.

PART TWO

MESSENGERS
OF GRACE

PEOPLE ARE BEAUTIFUL, courageous, and inspiring, but we are also messy, complicated, and fallible.

And yet we are dear to God's heart. In Genesis—the first book of both the Jewish Torah and the Christian Bible—we learn that all humanity is created in the image and likeness of God. The Qur'an teaches us that God (Allah) is "nearer to man than his jugular vein." In Catholic Social Teaching, the dignity of each person is the first principle. Quakers affirm there is "that of God in everyone."

Ever wonder why so many religious traditions feel the need to point this out?

I love how my friend John puts it: every person we meet contains a revelation of God.

In Matthew 25, Jesus says that whatever we do for "the least of these," we do for him. Who are these "least"? If we look at Jesus' list (people who are hungry, thirsty, naked, or ill, those who are strangers or imprisoned), we will see that he clearly identified with those who were most vulnerable.

Sometimes vulnerability is attractive, and sometimes it is repellent, but it is always a place where, if we cock our heads at a certain angle, we can catch the message God wants us to hear.

CHAPTER 8

Finding God in a Flowered Housedress

I have called you by name: you are mine.

—ISAIAH 43:1

ROSE WAS SCARY. AND SHE WAS SCARED.

She hovered in her bedroom doorway in a flowered, old-lady housedress and ratty slippers, her chopped-off hair looking like it had been styled in an asylum. Eyes full of suspicion, she peered anxiously at the do-gooders who had come to mess up her apartment. But it was that or eviction.

I was the head do-gooder, sent by Rose's social worker along with four of my students as part of an alternative spring break service experience. The apartment had descended into filth and chaos, we'd been told, since Rose's "boyfriend" had been transferred into assisted living. The landlord was ready to bounce her, so it was our job to make the place habitable—and not just for the many roaches scurrying through the cabinets.

I was so proud of my students that day. They donned gloves and tackled that awful kitchen with good cheer, emptying cabinets, throwing out contaminated food, and washing every sticky surface. I had the far easier task of organizing the living room: tossing discarded food wrappers, newspapers, and tissues; organizing anything that looked worth keeping; dusting everything I could get my hands on. There weren't as many roaches to be alarmed by, but there was Rose, watching me with alarm. She didn't respond to any overtures, so I went about my business quietly under her apprehensive gaze.

How is this her life? I found myself wondering. Having been blessed with what I considered a full and meaningful life, overflowing with friends and work, travel and adventures, I was increasingly distressed by the emptiness of this poor woman's existence.

And then I found it. Hidden among the junk mail and copies of *TV Guide* was a birthday card, the kind you get at a dollar store. I peeked inside.

My darling Rose, I will always love you.
— your Bill

My eyes welled up, and I gently placed the card in a prominent position on her freshly dusted end table. To me, she had seemed like a pathetic creature, yet she was someone's *darling Rose*. She was a social worker's challenging case, a landlord's problem tenant, and our Tuesday project, yet a man named Bill had remembered her birthday and had selected, written, and mailed this card with its tender message.

I do believe that we are all precious in the eyes of God. But I was humbled, that day, to realize that a person I could barely bring myself to look at was precious in the eyes of another human being—one who had penned the words we all long to hear.

Who do you find difficult to look at, never mind love? Try to imagine them as precious in the eyes of God, and even in the eyes of another human being. What shifts inside you?

CHAPTER 9

Finding God on the Phone

When you call me, and come and pray to me, I will listen to you.
—JEREMIAH 29:12

"I THINK I MIGHT BE CALLING MY MOTHER TOO MUCH," the young woman said on retreat.

Knowing that everyone's sense of "too much" is different, I asked her how often she and her mom typically talked.

"Oh, probably ten times," she said.

"Ten times a week *is* a lot," I replied.

"No," she exclaimed. "Ten times a day!"

She had crossed the country for a year of volunteer work after college and was living in a rough urban area, trying to create community with her housemates and doing work that was satisfying but immensely challenging. She had taken to chatting with her mother—on the opposite coast—as regularly as one might talk to a co-worker at the next desk, calling to update her on each joy and frustration she encountered in the course of her day.

How did her mom have time for all these phone calls? I first assumed that she was at home with younger children, but in fact, she ran her own business. She was a single mother, and it had always been just the two of them. So when her remarkable daughter went away for a year of service, she put her staff on notice: *If she calls, put her through, no questions asked, no matter what.*

I was still close enough to my own mother's death to begin to well up, knowing that I would never hear her voice on the phone again. And the counselor in me thought this young lady just might need a lesson in boundaries. But the conversation was not about me, and it wasn't therapy; it was spiritual direction. So I simply said, "You know, they say we first learn what God is like from our parents. Your mom has been a great model of God's care. I can almost hear God saying, 'If she prays, put her through, no questions asked, no matter what!'"

How good it is that the ways of God can be revealed in the people who care for us. And yet there is also something to be said for the old marketing phrase, *eliminate the middleman*—or, as a popular televangelist asks, "When you are upset, do you run to the phone or the Throne?"

So often, the people we run to for consolation when we're agitated only stir us up more. Personally, I know that having a sympathetic audience for the dramatic recitation of my angst only encourages me to hone my performance. That's why I need to learn to go to God first. Prayer purifies my thoughts, allowing less room for drama and self-pity. In God I find a ready listener, but also one who demands rigorous honesty and calls me to greater self-awareness and growth.

I can get away with so much more on the phone!

What problem in your life are you talking about right now? How are your friends or loved ones reacting? In the quiet, take it to God. Do you find yourself speaking of it differently? What do you hear in response?

CHAPTER 10

Finding God in Mercy

Have mercy on me, God, in accord with your merciful love.
—PSALM 51:3

HER NAME WAS MELODY, and her tune was sadder than a country song in a minor key. She was young and homeless, sobbing and shaking, badly beaten up and outrageously drunk. And deciding what to do with her fell to me.

Did I mention that it was only ten in the morning?

I had been the administrative assistant at the Street Center for just a few months, but our director was away, and the social workers who shared the building with us were in a long staff meeting. So around and around and around the block Melody and I walked. I tried to talk her into going to the police station for help. I tried to talk her *out* of going to the liquor store for more Wild Irish Rose. Finally, I persuaded her to sleep it off on our office couch, instead.

Thirty years later, I can still remember how moved I was as I watched her relax in that safe space. I remember how heartsick I felt when she woke up and went straight back to the guy who had just lost his temper all over her face. And I keenly remember how much trouble I got in when the head social worker discovered what I had done.

Didn't I know that clients (whom our agency called guests) were not allowed in the building visibly drunk? Didn't I know that the professionals were aware of Melody's situation? Didn't I know that sometimes people needed to hit rock bottom for a change to occur?

In retrospect, I can see it from her perspective: I was a twenty-two-year-old suburban girl with zero social work training, undoing her work while her back was turned.

Yet I'm pretty sure I would do it again.

I work for a university sponsored by the Sisters of Mercy now, and find myself in a lot of conversations about what mercy means. The simplest definition I hear is *meet the need*, which, as I understood it that day, was a good dose of kindness and a safe place to sleep. (And for the record, when my director got back to the building, he vigorously affirmed my choice.)

I've also heard that mercy means *giving someone the break they don't deserve.* But here's the thing: we rarely deserve it. Who among us hasn't messed up, said or done things that still make us cringe, or hurt people we love? Who hasn't needed a little tenderness before the tough love could sink in? The only difference is that Melody's private drama was enacted on a public stage, mostly for lack of a safety net.

No one *merits* mercy; it flows from the heart of God, freely, to each of us. How can we be stingy when we have the opportunity to share it?

When have you given someone a break he or she did not deserve? When have you received such a break? Who needs your mercy today?

CHAPTER 11

Finding God in My Arms

O Most High, when I am afraid, in you I place my trust.
—PSALM 56:3-4

THE DINING HALL WAS BUZZING WITH ACTIVITY. It was almost time for the mothers' weekly support group meeting, but first, we had to organize the children. They had wolfed down the peanut butter and jelly sandwiches we'd made. Now, with full tummies and sticky mouths, they were being divided into groups so my students could entertain them with age-appropriate activities while their mothers met.

So far, this probably sounds like the sort of cheerful scene that could be unfolding anywhere. But we were just north of the Mexican border in Laredo, Texas, and the mothers were residents and recent graduates of a local domestic violence shelter.

They had escaped poverty in their own countries and abuse in their own homes, and had found refuge here, in the care of the Sisters of Mercy. For these mothers, the support group might well have been called a survival group.

Most of them had already released their energetic youngsters to the play activities when one thin woman caught my attention. She was hovering at the edge of the room, carrying a sleeping toddler who appeared to grow heavier by the minute. I approached her and asked, in tentative Spanish, "Do you want me to take care of your boy?" She hesitated a moment, then smiled gratefully. "Rodrigo," she said, transferring him into my arms. Cradling him carefully, I made my way to the baby room and sank into an armchair without waking him. The only other occupant of the room was an elderly Mexican woman with a sleeping infant. She placed her charge softly in one of the playpens and gestured for me to do the same, but I couldn't bring myself to put Rodrigo down.

Is there anything more wonderful than the weight of a child sound asleep in your arms? I do know that an exhausted toddler can crash anywhere, but to my heart that afternoon, Rodrigo's slumber represented not just deep sleep, but deep trust. Conscious that I could not imagine what trauma he might have experienced in his short life, I tried to be as still as possible, to spare him the shock of falling asleep in his mother's arms and waking up with a total stranger.

Looking down at his sweet face, I thought of all the kids in my own family, and of the secure and joyful childhoods they were experiencing, as they should be, as *he* should be. I thought of Rodrigo's mom, who had taken great risks to get him to safety, and of the Sisters and volunteers at the shelter and even the other mothers, all striving to help her create a decent life for her boy. I thought of Saint Teresa of Avila's words: *Christ has no body now but yours.* So many good people were trying to be the hands and feet of God for this child. *Keep him safe through them,* I prayed. *Keep him safe!*

Imagine cradling the earth in your arms, with all its beauty and distress. What stirs your compassion? Where are you called to embody God's love? How will you respond?

CHAPTER 12

Finding God in the Cafeteria

How precious to me are your designs, O God; how vast the sum of them.
—Psalm 139:17

*H*ow did you get started in public speaking? The question came at the end of a presentation I had just given in a parish cafeteria in front of almost a hundred women. I chuckled as I realized that the answer had begun when I was a tongue-tied teenager in another cafeteria, almost forty years earlier.

It was the first day of high school, and my family had just moved into the neighborhood. I was terribly shy and didn't know a soul, while most of the other students had arrived with classmates from their grade schools. I was assigned to third-period lunch but had no idea where to sit, so I just stood there, lost amid a chattering mass of ponytails and perms.

Suddenly, a face came into focus right in front of me. *I noticed you were in my first two classes,* the girl said. *Would you like to sit together?*

Kathy—still one of my dearest friends—does not remember that moment, though I've retold the story countless times in her presence. But for me, our encounter was a pivot; it altered my path dramatically, in more ways than one. Kath was joining the speech and debate team because her big sister was on it. I was happy to follow my new friend anywhere, so I joined, too, and spent the next four years honing my speaking skills in competition and on stage. I located my voice, and now I preach, perform, even sing in front of crowds. Where would the road-not-taken have led? I don't know, and I don't want to. I do know that I will never stop thanking my friend for her moment of spontaneous generosity. I am writing this on Kathy's fifty-second birthday, praying that joy will continue to come her way in as much measure as her kindness brought me.

I am not an "everything happens for a reason" kind of person, but I do think it works in reverse. When we trace a wonderful thing in our life back through each twist and turn that could have gone another way, there's a good chance we will discover something we wished had been different at the time. I would not have chosen to be the lonely kid in the cafeteria, but my vulnerability set the stage God needed for a new invitation.

No amount of subsequent grace can make up for genuine tragedy, but the truth is that many of the good things in our lives would not have been possible without some of the bad. Think of an undreamed-of second marriage following the untimely death of a beloved spouse. I imagine God at work like a seasoned quilter, using the scraps and sorrows, the false starts and failed attempts of our lives to create something beautiful.

I can only bow before the mystery.

Pick a joy in your life and trace it back as far as you can. What sorrow do you find there that the joy would not have been possible without? Don't try to make sense of it; just bow before the mystery.

CHAPTER 13

Finding God in Smoky Fur

The Lord is close to the brokenhearted.

—Psalm 34:19

D OG PERSON OR CAT PERSON? It's an easy conversation starter. As someone who grew up with dogs, I never thought I would struggle to answer it. When I was a busy young apartment-dweller, however, a cat adopted me, and kept me company well into my middle age. Consequently, I came to appreciate the subtle virtues of a feline friend.

On the day after Christmas many years ago, I returned from my parents' house, dragging my presents up two flights of stairs. I fed Delilah, and then, fully intending to put everything away, lit an evergreen-scented pillar candle in the living room and began puttering. Unpacking the gifts, I glanced at a book called *Dogspell* that my dad had given me. It was about the ways our canine companions mirror God's unconditional love. Drawn in by the first page, I went from reading the book standing in the hallway to reading it sitting on the edge of the bed to reading it lying down.

Presently, Delilah joined me, as she often did. She jumped onto my legs, and then walked up the length of my body, settling on my chest and butting against my chin. I kissed the top of her furry head. "You smell funny," I murmured absentmindedly. "Why do you smell funny?" Suddenly, she had my attention. "Why do you smell like *smoke?*" Then I remembered the candle.

Sure enough, in the living room, my forgotten candle had cracked down the side, spilling hot wax all over the television and rug. A dried corsage nearby had caught fire and been consumed. I have no idea how much more damage would have been done if I had fallen asleep.

Unlike Lassie, a cat cannot come barking in to tell you Timmy's down the well. But Delilah got my attention in her own quiet way. *Something is very wrong in the next room*, she communicated. *Smell my fur!*

There is wisdom here for all of us. If we say we care about people who are suffering, we can't keep our distance; we need to draw close. We have to immerse ourselves in others' reality, near enough to tell what's really going on. It's like what Pope Francis told his priests: *Shepherds should carry the smell of their sheep.*

Can I say how little that appeals to me? I don't even like it when someone wearing cologne hugs me and I catch the scent in my hair for the rest of the day.

Yet we cannot insulate ourselves from others, hiding behind the illusory barriers of our differences. Too many people's lives are on fire. If we happen to have been born in the next room, we can't rest in comfort while our sisters and brothers are burning. We need to get close enough to understand their pain before we can work to alleviate it. *Get closer,* God beckons. *Smell my fur.*

Whose suffering would you rather not "smell"? What is one thing you can do to draw closer?

CHAPTER 14

Finding God on the Oncology Floor

What will separate us from the love of Christ?
—ROMANS 8:35

IN MY YEAR AS A YOUNG HOSPITAL CHAPLAIN, I met many patients, but there was one in particular whose faith still inspires me.

I'd been paged to the oncology floor late on a Sunday afternoon. The nurse said one of her patients was Catholic, and would like to receive Communion. Inwardly, I groaned; it was not a Catholic hospital, so the in-house chaplains didn't have access to the sacrament, and the Communion ministers from the local parish had come and gone hours ago. I didn't know why this woman had been overlooked, but now it was my job to go disappoint her.

And yet she was not disappointed. Rosemarie greeted me warmly and shrugged off my apology. It was okay; could we just visit, instead? I realized I'd been stereotyping her during my long walk through the corridors. In my imagination, she was the sort of Catholic who would be mystified at how a twenty-five-year-old woman could possibly be the chaplain (as, frankly, I was still a bit mystified myself).

She told me her medical story in brief, and it was as sad a tale as one would expect to hear on that floor. A mother of young children, she had been losing her battle with an aggressive cancer and now was pursuing a radical experimental treatment.

Then she told me her faith story. A lukewarm cradle Catholic, Rosemarie had been invited by a neighbor to her parish's charismatic prayer group when she got sick. She went, at first, because she was willing to try anything; it was the spiritual equivalent of her clinical trial. Yet over time, her experience of direct encounter with God in prayer was profoundly life-changing. It grounded her in something deeper and more eternal than whatever was happening on the oncology ward.

"The cancer will do what the cancer will do," Rosemarie announced. "But what has happened in my relationship with God, I would not trade for anything."

This may be the greatest profession of faith I've ever heard outside the Bible.

In his *Spiritual Exercises*, Saint Ignatius wrote that we should not prefer health or sickness, wealth or poverty, success or failure, a long life or a short one. It sounds crazy, I know; how could regular people in the world be that detached from their own fate? But Ignatius insisted that *everything* "has the potential of calling forth in us a deeper response to our life in God." I have studied that passage, prayed with it, and taught it, but Rosemarie was *living* it, despite—or perhaps because of—circumstances that would make most people despair of God's goodness.

My encounter with Rosemarie taught me to hold my own future more lightly. While health, wealth, success, and longevity still sound preferable to the alternatives, her perspective has stayed with me, giving flesh to the bones of Ignatius' beloved prayer: "Give me only your love and your grace; that's enough for me."

When have you been able to hold your future lightly? What circumstances challenge your ability to do that? Try praying the prayer of Saint Ignatius. What happens?

Part Three

FAR FROM HOME

In Genesis 12, God said to Abram: *Go forth from your land, your relatives, and from your father's house to a land that I will show you.* With that line, the curtain rose for all three "Abrahamic" traditions: Judaism, Christianity, and Islam.

Why did Abraham (as he was eventually called) have to leave home?

Setting aside geographical concerns, God needed Abram to practice radical trust: to go beyond everything he knew and almost everyone who had his back, and set off for an as-yet-undisclosed location. (Like Outward Bound, but without the crampons and carabiners.)

The plain truth is that there are things we cannot learn from inside our comfort zone: things about the world around us, yes, but especially things about ourselves. Whenever we venture into another culture, country, or continent, we often experience a disorienting shift in our perspective. If we're lucky, it's permanent.

Travel changes us for the better, especially when we are willing to open ourselves to what God wants us to unlearn.

Bon voyage!

CHAPTER 15

Finding God on Holy Ground

Remove your sandals from your feet, for the place where you stand is holy ground.
—Exodus 3:5

WHEN I VISITED UNIVERSITIES IN SOUTH AMERICA one summer with campus ministers from the United States, our trip across Peru included a visit to Machu Picchu, the Lost City of the Incas. Undiscovered and consequently unharmed by Spanish conquistadores, this abandoned city was obscured by thick jungle until the early 1900s. Now a prime tourist destination, it nevertheless retains an air of mystery.

From the picturesque city of Cuzco, we journeyed by train through the Andes, arriving at the village of Aguas Calientes in a downpour. Surrounded at once by vendors of treasures, trinkets, and rain ponchos, we boarded a shuttle that crept up a long switchback road, emerging into brilliant sunshine above the cloud line. (Glad I hadn't purchased a poncho!) A seemingly endless guided tour of the ruins followed, made longer by everyone's desire to be off on their own. Finally given free time, we scattered across the sacred site in search of solitude. Alone at last in the most beautiful place I had ever been, I looked for a good spot to pray.

I settled into an isolated outcropping with a spectacular view, but my soul was not settled. I tried to pray, but my mind began to race. What was I doing with my life? I was thirty-six, eight years into my job, dwelling with two cats on the third floor of an old house. My life was busy, fulfilling, and prayerful, but somehow, I felt I was not living up to the promise I had shown in college and grad school. How did God feel about all this? Was I on the right path, or had I missed a turn? Was I doing God's will, or was I letting God down?

Suddenly, I was struck by the conviction that this train of thought would not stop at any useful stations. A sentence materialized in my mind, as clearly as if God had spoken aloud: *If you want to know how much I love you, look around!*

I was touched, but I still wasn't sure. What if I'd made that up? No sooner had this doubt entered my mind than I spotted a hummingbird just a few feet away. It hovered for a moment, looked right at me, and flew off. I'd only seen a few of these miniature wonders in my life, but they always carried a message of divine consolation. I quit fussing and relaxed into prayer before God's astounding creation.

If you want to know how much I love you, look around. Machu Picchu is a sacred site, but I shouldn't have to travel so far from home to hear God's words of love. I can connect with God in a quiet church, at my favorite park, in a beautiful garden, or even in my own backyard, warmed by the setting sun on a cool afternoon. Holy ground abounds. I should take off my sandals more often.

What place is "holy ground" for you? Take yourself there, in person or in imagination. Be still, and listen for what God wants to tell you.

CHAPTER 16

Finding God in an Outstretched Hand

For where your treasure is, there also will your heart be.

—LUKE 12:34

HOW DO WE DECIDE WHAT TO GIVE?
In my years as a campus minister, I've been fortunate to travel to Mexico City with students many times. One of the problems for the tourist there (as for urban pedestrians just about anywhere) is how to respond to people who are begging. So often in Mexico City, I encountered tiny crones sitting on the sidewalk, wrapped in dirty blankets, heads down in sleep or shame, one calloused hand extended for passersby to see. They gave no accusing stare to those who passed them by; they didn't confront us with a fast-talking pitch or a conscience-prodding sign. They simply sat immobile

for hours, murmuring heart-wrenching blessings to strangers who paused to press a coin into their palms.

On my first visit, I'd often found myself unprepared to give: the airport currency exchange had doled out maddeningly large bills, difficult to break at local shops. The next time, I secured a supply of ten-peso coins. Each was worth about a dollar; they were easy to carry in my pocket (unlike bills that had to be extricated from my travel wallet) and satisfying to bestow—a nice, solid coin. I roamed about the Basilica of Our Lady of Guadalupe like a trippy fairy godmother, never passing one of those dear old souls without giving a coin and receiving a blessing in return.

Was that praiseworthy? If I compare giving to *not* giving, sure. But if I compare what I *had*, even on my person, to what those ladies *needed*…ugh. The logical part of me protests that even if I had emptied my bank account (that is, sold everything I had and given to the poor), I might have had treasure in heaven, but there would still be an awful lot of poor widows in Mexico City. Yet that observation, however true, does nothing to un-complicate my feelings about my peso-giving choices. Nor should it.

Whenever students and I talk about this, I first make sure they understand that the systemic and sociological factors at work in poverty are vast and complicated, but can be addressed. (Perhaps one of them will graduate and do just that.) Then I explain the biblical concept of tithing (giving the first ten percent of one's income back to

God in some way), and encourage them to support charities which address underlying causes as well as immediate needs. I let them know that, whatever they decide, the important thing is that they respond thoughtfully.

And finally, I take away any tidy bow they were hoping to tie on the lesson by telling them this: from a spiritual perspective, we should never grow comfortable with the discomfort of others—even when we feel like we're down to our last two coins.

How do you practice generosity? More importantly, how do you practice staying uncomfortable with the reality of this world's inequities?

CHAPTER 17

Finding God in Uncertainty

Do not boast about tomorrow, for you do not know what any day may bring forth.
—Proverbs 27:1

IT WAS ALWAYS SO HARD TO SAY GOODBYE.
Each winter break for several years, I brought students on a "working pilgrimage" to Mexico City, where we stayed with an amazing host family. Abuelita Inocencia was the matriarch; her daughters, sons-in-law, and grandkids were forever in and out of each other's homes, celebrating innumerable special occasions, laughing and joking, and offering such generous hospitality. The more time I spent with them, the more I came to dread those airport partings.

I would try to soften the blow in what I now understand was a typically American fashion. A day or two before our scheduled departure, I would start to lay out plans for the next visit—often a year away. No one ever took me up on it. No one got out their calendars or said, *oh, yes, that will be great,* or *next year we'll have to try such-and-such,* or even *please bring more Spanish-speaking students next time!* Instead, they always smiled indulgently, like I was a child mispronouncing a word, and uttered the same enigmatic phrase: "*primero Dios.*" Literally: *first, God.* A bit like our occasional "God willing," *primero Dios* was sprinkled like salt through every conversation.

I remembered the concept but had forgotten the phrase, so I tried to retrieve it recently by Facebook-messaging with the oldest granddaughter in an awkward mixture of English and Spanish. Not quite understanding what I was looking for, Vero gave me a couple explanations about the importance of putting things in God's hands, then moved on to family updates. Could I believe that in just three years—*primero Dios*—they would be celebrating her baby sister's *quinceañera* (the grand fifteenth-birthday party)?

Aha!

I think my host family uses *primero Dios* reflexively because they don't take as much for granted as I do. Displayed in their living room are professional photos of each child in a fancy outfit at his or her *presentación,* the third-birthday extravaganza. The tradition dates back to a time when many children died in infancy, and reaching age three was really something to celebrate.

Even though infant mortality in Mexico is greatly improved, the people carry that uncertainty in their bones. Consequently, my hosts did not tempt fate with presumptive words. While the family certainly hoped I would return, they refused to entertain my scheming about the next visit because they understood it as a gift, not a guarantee. And, of course, they were right.

If you want to make God laugh, tell him your plans, we joke here in the States. And yet we keep making them, acting like we're in charge of our fate, grousing when things don't go our way, prioritizing stuff that doesn't matter, and postponing joy like there's every tomorrow.

Primero Dios.

Try to think of one assumption you are unconsciously making about your future. Is there anything you would do differently now if you really understood that it was not certain?

CHAPTER 18

Finding God in Forgiveness

As the Lord has forgiven you, so must you also do.
—COLOSSIANS 3:13

TIM WAS SO SICK. We were in Mexico City for our annual service-immersion experience—eight college students and two campus ministers—and on the final day, Tim went down hard. Perhaps it was the water, but more likely it was the way he had hurdled the language barrier with the men in our host family by eating every food they dared him to, no matter how spicy or unidentifiable. Twenty-four hours before we were due to fly home, our host grandmother, Inocencia, took Tim to the doctor, who gave him a shot of something and instructions to continue the injections every six hours.

At 2:00 A.M., twelve hours before flight time, Inocencia got up to give Tim his next shot. But we couldn't find the syringes! We searched frantically, and even woke up Tim's roommate, Mark, to ask if he had seen them, to no avail. Since Tim was so sick and flight time so close, Inocencia asked her son-in-law Luis to drive her to get more syringes at a 24-hour pharmacy some distance away.

Luis's car had barely disappeared around the corner when Mark stumbled sleepily into the kitchen. "Is this what you were looking for?" he asked, holding up the missing box. Apparently, he had decided to be helpful and pack the communal suitcase a few hours earlier, and had thrown in everything he thought was ours—including the syringes.

Now the wait began. This was before cell phones. We had no way of contacting Ino and Luis, and they were gone for a very long time. Mark sat at the kitchen table looking just as miserable as Tim. Our students adored this host family, and the realization that his careless mistake had sent these dear people out into the city in the middle of the night weighed on Mark terribly. Finally, the door opened, and as they walked in, Mark guiltily held out the box, braced for their reaction.

I was watching their faces, and what I saw was amazing. There was not even a fleeting trace of annoyance. There was nothing that suggested they were glad we were leaving in eleven hours. There was only laughter, and giving Tim his shot.

By breakfast, Tim was much better, but Mark was still a mess. "I can't believe I did that," he said. "They were so good about it. How can I ever repay them?" I told him what I knew to be true: he couldn't. "Mark, you have just experienced the kind of utter forgiveness that most of us only get from God. All you can do is be grateful, and remember this feeling the next time someone offends *you*." (Mark is a police officer now, and recently told me he frequently recalls that lesson.)

So much human forgiveness is partial, grudging, or conditional. No wonder we have a hard time imagining the fullness of God's mercy. Isn't it ironic that the only way to catch a glimpse is to stand in need of it?

In prayer, try to hold one of your faults before God without minimizing or rationalizing, and express your sorrow in simple, heartfelt words. Can you hear God's gentle, joyful response?

CHAPTER 19

Finding God in a Foreign Tongue

Therefore, I will allure her now;
I will lead her into the wilderness and speak persuasively to her.
Por eso, ahora la voy a conquistar, la llevaré al desierto y allí le hablaré con su corazón.
—Hosea/Oseas 2:16

I HAVE NEVER TRAVELED IN A COUNTRY where I didn't speak at least a bit of the language.

It started off easy. The first three countries I visited were all in Latin America, where my five years of Spanish classes served me well. Being able to navigate all those metros and menus had a downside, however: it made me reluctant to travel anywhere I *didn't* speak the language. Not wanting to stay home, I just enlarged my linguistic comfort zone. In preparation for a week in Montreal, I immersed myself in beginner

French for months. Knowing I'd be spending five days in Italy during our cruise, I listened to learn-Italian podcasts for half a year.

Can you say overkill? (Can you say it in more than one language?)

At first, my resolution was purely self-protective—a pashmina of vocabulary to maintain the illusion of control. But then I began to notice the joy. Every language has its own nuance, flair, and words that just sound better than their equivalent in English. Finding a splendid new phrase in my mouth was like biting into a warm *churro:* I savored it, and immediately wanted more.

The real pleasure, of course, was not the words themselves, but their ability to bridge the divide between strangers. I still remember the first time I spontaneously cracked a joke in Spanish with my Mexican host family. The joke itself is long gone, but the memory of Luis bursting into laughter on the sidewalk remains. I loved the feeling of connection that grew each time we were able to really understand each other.

Despite my forays into French and Italian, Spanish is my first love; I call it the language of my soul. When I am able to pray in Spanish, I sometimes connect with God even better.

In the biblical story of Martha and Mary, for example (Luke 10:38-42), Jesus tells Martha, "You are anxious and worried about many things." In my Spanish Bible, it's *te pierdes en mil cosas*—literally, "You lose yourself in a thousand things." That describes my own distractedness so much better than simply "anxious and worried." Or take a prayer of Saint Teresa of Avila that I've loved since childhood: in English, we say, "God alone suffices," but Teresa herself said *solo Dios basta*: a precise translation, but more vigorous and satisfying to pronounce.

Ironically, it is probably my lack of fluency that makes prayer in Spanish so powerful for me. Not having a thesaurus or dissertation running in my head helps me stay focused on the words right in front of me. Keeping whole areas of my mind out of the conversation enables my prayer to be simpler, more grounded in feelings than in thoughts. What a relief it must be for God to murmur directly to my heart, instead of engaging in the usual protracted negotiations with my busy brain!

Is there a word in another language that helps you to connect with God? If languages aren't your thing, try simply changing the posture you pray in. Any alternative that bypasses your brain can lead to a more direct encounter with the divine.

CHAPTER 20

Finding God in the Grikes

But some seed fell on rich soil, and produced fruit, a hundred or sixty or thirtyfold.
—MATTHEW 13:8

MY FAMILY TOOK GREAT PRIDE IN BEING FROM THE EMERALD ISLE, so when my brother and I had a chance to do our first grown-up vacation together, of course we headed to Ireland. Everyone always raves about how green the countryside is, but soon after landing, we found ourselves driving across the Burren, where a terrain of ghostly limestone stretched out ten miles in front of us. What the heck?

Derived from the Gaelic word for "stony place," the Burren was described more than three centuries ago as a land where there is "not enough water to drown a man, wood enough to hang him, nor earth enough to bury him." From a distance, the landscape appeared stark, but the innkeeper who gave us directions had been insistent—this was what we had to see. So we got out and started walking.

It seems as though the Burren should be a barren place, but up close, it is shockingly fertile. Out of the grikes (cracks in the limestone), flowers bloom with abandon. It's like a finding a conservatory on the moon.

I was deeply moved by the abundance of life in such a bleak place. How were all these flowers being fed? The answer, of course, is pretty simple: it's not the quantity, but the *quality* of nourishment that's essential in the Burren. In other words, for that smidge of soil down in the grikes to support such life, it has to be one magnificent bit of dirt.

My favorite photo from that day is a close-up of a rock. Out of a hole no more than two inches wide springs a veritable salad bowl of miniature greens: ferns, fronds, and even a tiny flower. I keep the picture as a reminder of how I want my spirit to be, regardless of my surroundings.

Every once in a while, I'll meet someone who makes me think, *how are you possibly thriving in this environment? What is the source of your joy under such harsh circumstances?* Obviously, this person has roots plunged into the right stuff.

So, what is that stuff? Some would call it faith. Yet I know plenty of churchgoers who, in times of adversity, seem not the least bit consoled by what they profess. I want to be anchored in a faith that sustains me no matter what, a nourishing faith that lets me strive for good things without being attached to a specific outcome.

Though I am blessed by dear relatives, marvelous friends, and fulfilling work, I know how easily any of that could be taken from me. That's why the faith I crave is confidence in God alone. Like the life in the grikes, I want to dig my roots deep into that which is eternal: the rich source of my serenity.

What are you agitated about right now? In prayer, envision stretching your roots down into God's fertile soil. Imagine drawing up into yourself the peace, strength, and balance you need to meet the day.

CHAPTER 21

Finding God at My Feet

If I, therefore, the master and teacher, have washed your feet,
you ought to wash one another's feet.

—JOHN 13:14

"SHINE YOUR SHOES, LADY?"

I was in Nuevo Laredo, Mexico, just south of Laredo, Texas, where I was leading a week of spring break service. My students and I were headed back to the border after experiencing the infamous bridge crossing—Mexicans going one way to work, Americans going the other way to shop. And at the moment, I was busy pretending not to hear the fellow calling out to me from the street corner.

I am not a person who gets shoeshines. Having bad feet, I buy footwear that's as practical and supportive as a good friend. And because I accept (yet resent) the fact that I am never going to skip around in pretty little flats or sexy stilettos, I generally ignore my shoes unless they hurt. But there was no ignoring this persistent young man.

"Shine your shoes?" he called again, literally running with his shoeshine kit down the block to catch up with me. "Look at your shoes!" he cried. "I'll shine them fast, good price!" Only then did I glance at my sturdy black boots. Scuffed and dusty, they looked like something I'd fished out of a dumpster. The man had a point. I acquiesced, and he went to work—right in the middle of the sidewalk.

I was mortified. Standing there with four of my students while this young Mexican man knelt at my feet for what seemed like an eternity, I felt as conspicuous as if I had purchased a giant sombrero with the words *frivolous American* embroidered across the brim. Unaccustomed to being served in this manner, I prayed that no one had a camera.

Then I noticed something. He was doing a really good job. He polished and buffed vigorously; he was in the *zone*. The man was a professional, doing his job with flair and efficiency. My shoes had never looked better—even right out of the box.

As a further mortification, I needed to borrow money from a student to pay him—a "good price" being higher than I had expected, but worth every peso.

What lingers from that encounter is confusion about my own discomfort. The inequality I experienced as the young man knelt at my feet could have gone either way. On the one hand, I was a tourist "rich" enough to hire someone to do this menial task for me, and he was a laborer stuck hustling business in the street. But to leave it there would be to deny the dignity of work and worker. To be on the receiving end of his skill was humbling, for he was a good shoe-shiner, and I am a crummy one. He deserved his good price, and my respect. I'm glad he got both.

Think of the many people who provide services for you (trash collector, grocery clerk) and hold them in prayer, one by one. How do you show your gratitude for their good work, and respect for their dignity as children of God?

PART FOUR

WORKING IT OUT

Psalm 139 says, *I praise you, for I am fearfully and wonderfully made.* Even that joyful line from one of the most consoling psalms makes it clear: we are complicated. *Life* is complicated.

Growing up (and sometimes well beyond), we struggle to know ourselves—to understand our identity, name our gifts, believe we are lovable, and discover our call. Life brings great joys but also crushing sorrows, of which some people seem to have more than their share. We go about uncertain of our choices, frustrated by our imperfections, bent by grief, yet deeply desiring to make sense of it all.

Where is God in all this? That's the great question of the spiritual life. The important thing, however, is not to answer it definitively, but to keep asking the question. In *Star Wars*, Yoda says, "Do. Or do not. There is no try." With apologies to that adorable wisdom figure, in the spiritual life, there is always "try."

My mother taught religion to high school boys for twenty-five years. She knew that their hours in her class would be among their last in formal religious instruction, so she made sure they understood that learning about God did not stop at the classroom door. Life, she said, is basically theology lab.

May *your* lab work be a constant source of amazement!

CHAPTER 22

Finding God in Irreverence

And Jesus wept.
—JOHN 11:35

THE YOUNG MOTHER IN THE EMERGENCY ROOM was rushed there straight from her son's christening party. She had been diagnosed with cancer while she was pregnant, and had postponed treatment for several months until the baby was delivered safely. Now, instead of rejoicing with her guests, she found herself in a frightening place: suffering with a high fever *and* knowing that she might not live to celebrate her boy's first birthday.

For a long time, she seemed to want nothing to do with me, but her situation was so sad that I pushed myself to stay longer than I ordinarily would with someone unreceptive. Finally, something seemed to shift in her, and she said, "You're nicer than the last chaplain I talked to here."

Uh-oh.

Then she told me about her recent encounter with one of my colleagues, who had "consoled" her by saying, "Just remember that what you are going through is as nothing compared to what Jesus suffered on the cross."

For a moment, I couldn't breathe.

How could anyone say that, especially to this courageous woman, who might have just sacrificed her own life for her child's? At a time when she most needed to feel God's consoling presence, a minister had turned her Savior into a distant, judgmental, even competitive figure. How could I make this right?

Pious words wouldn't do; she'd had quite enough of those. I braced myself and offered what may still be my best pastoral response, even after all these years: "*Did you tell that chaplain that Jesus was only on the cross for three hours, and he didn't have kids?*"

For a moment, *she* didn't breathe. Then she burst out laughing until tears ran down her face. The conversation that ensued was profound. The chasm left by the other chaplain had been bridged by sincerity and humor.

My words may have been irreverent, but they came from a very reverent place—the certainty that our God is compassion and love.

Is there a pious expression or concept that leaves you cold? How would you reframe it? When has a tragedy challenged you to think through what you really believe about God? Where did you land?

CHAPTER 23

Finding God in Imperfection

But we hold this treasure in earthen vessels,
that the surpassing power may be of God and not from us.
—2 CORINTHIANS 4:7

JUST AS MAJOR LEAGUE PITCHERS DREAM OF THE PERFECT GAME, cantors long for the perfect service. Most of the glitches that bedevil us go unnoticed by the congregation, I'm sure. Yet how I long to finish just one liturgy without a single bad note, missed cue, late entrance, abandoned harmony, wrong word, or miscommunication with the piano player!

I almost made it one Sunday. But then, at the very end of the recessional hymn, our pianist cued me to repeat the refrain. Guessing her transition wrong, I came in too soon the second time. As I cringed and tried again four beats later, I realized that this was my first and only mistake of the Mass. On the spectrum of failures in life, it was barely worth citing. Still, I was annoyed with myself.

As I sang the refrain for the final time, however, I remembered one of my favorite sayings: "Only God is perfect." Repeating it like a mantra, I was able to let go of my aggravation and recapture a bit of equanimity.

It's a delicate balance, striving for perfection without being obsessed by it or undone when we fall short. I have heard that makers of both Persian rugs and Amish quilts sometimes deliberately leave one tiny flaw in their work as a humble acknowledgement that only God is perfect. I admire such honesty, even as I struggle against it. How different would my daily life be if the hamster wheel in my brain did not always start to spin every time I finished a task, conscious that I could have done it better? More importantly, how much more peaceful would I be if my hastily spoken words or omissions of charity (what I have done, and what I have failed to do) stirred contrition in my soul *without* sending my harsh internal critic into high gear?

Saint Francis de Sales was both clear and consoling on this topic. "We must not fret over our imperfections," he wrote in his *Introduction to the Devout Life.* When we discover a fault, we should simply say, "Alas, my poor heart, here we are, fallen into the pit we were so firmly resolved to avoid...let us start out again on the way of humility."

I wonder if this is one of the things Saint Paul was talking about when he told the Corinthians, "We hold this treasure in earthen vessels, that the surpassing power may be of God and not from us." How much pride would be at work in us if we achieved perfection on a regular basis? How little would we grasp our need for God?

I still hope for that perfect Mass. But since God chooses to use this "earthen vessel" to lead the congregation in song, I will strive to let the music flow with gratitude and a fair dose of humility, instead.

Which of your imperfections bothers you the most? As you hold it in mind, try to imagine yourself as a simple clay vessel in God's hands. How are you well used by God, just as you are?

CHAPTER 24

Finding God in Failure

My grace is sufficient for you, for power is made perfect in weakness.
—2 CORINTHIANS 12:9

"I WAS MARRIED BEFORE," she said. "Almost no one here knows."
And then it was her turn to be shocked, as I replied, "So was I!"

We had known each other for over a decade, and considered ourselves friends. How were we just learning this now?

It was *shame*, of course. We both traveled in religious circles, and were perceived to be good, moral women. While we knew that to be true, we also feared that people might look at us differently if they knew we'd been divorced, albeit a lifetime ago. So while we never *lied* about it, we also never talked about it.

As soon as she and I stepped into the fresh air of compassion and understanding, however, we felt our spirits rise and our friendship deepen. It became clear that either of us gladly would have spoken of our troubled past as soon as the other opened the door, but our mutual reluctance to *go first* had cost us ten years. That's a pretty high price to pay for an untarnished reputation.

People love stumbling on a commonality with one another; that's why we enjoy talking about our likes and dislikes, our quirks, and even our losses. If you are afraid of balloons or a fan of *Battlestar Galactica*, I can't wait to compare notes. If you're an introvert, a migraine sufferer, or a person who can't hack perfume, I'm eager to commiserate. If you've lost a parent recently, or you're accompanying a loved one through chemo or hospice, I'm grateful for the chance to connect as one who's been there.

But through each of us runs a current of shame connected to failure, and shame is isolating. The things I am ashamed of keep me silent—often with those who most need to hear the unedited story.

The truth is, life is messy for all of us. We make mistakes—often dreadful ones—and hurt each other badly. We overestimate our abilities and fall flat on our faces. Addictive behaviors resurface despite our sincerest resolutions. As Saint Paul told the Romans, "I do not do what I want, but I do what I hate" (7:15).

Yet our failures don't have to define us. Grace happens. Mercy is restorative. And that is a story worth telling. (Which is why the comeback kid is an inspiration, while the one who always gets it right the first time is just annoying.)

That *aha* moment with my friend helped me to see the less admirable parts of my story as gifts to be shared rather than embarrassments to be hidden. They are a testament to God's power to call forth goodness and create something beautiful in the wake of destruction. Telling the truth about it is a pretty small price to pay.

What in your past causes you shame? Have you also experienced some healing? What would it be like to take a risk and share your story? Who might benefit?

CHAPTER 25

Finding God in the YES

Do to others whatever you would have them do to you.
—Matthew 7:12

W HEN I WAS SIXTEEN YEARS OLD, I had my first summer job, conducting telephone surveys. It was awful. Each night, the company paid me $3.35 an hour to cold-call and mostly get hung up on by angry people all over the country. *Didn't I know it was dinnertime? Didn't I know they were having a thunderstorm?* Even the good folks who were willing to talk to me needed to fit a strict set of criteria: they had to be heads of households with children between ages seven and twelve, *and* one of those children also had to be available to interview. (I still find it hard to believe that seven is the age of reason.) To make matters worse, the full survey took twenty minutes to complete—all to better understand the usage patterns of steak sauce!

I wasn't very good at the job. I got at least one talking-to about my low call-completion rate, and according to the Social Security Administration, I made only $202 the whole summer. There was just one good thing that came out of it: I left that place with permanent compassion for survey-takers. I resolved always to say yes if one called or approached me, and to this day, I have never turned anyone away.

That resolution was put to the test one afternoon during a long drive up I-95, when I got off the highway to resolve a problem that too much hydration had created. I had just hustled into an unfamiliar mall, desperate to locate a ladies' room, when a smiling woman with a clipboard got me in her sights. Could she have just a few minutes of my time? I gritted my teeth, remembered my phone-bank days, and said yes. "We're taking a survey about toilet paper," she said. "Would you mind stepping over here and using this private bathroom?"

It was a karmic slam-dunk. (I can't make this stuff up.)

Now before I start in on the power of YES, let me acknowledge that under different circumstances, I very much believe in the power of NO. When it comes to the big things, we have to be intentional about how we spend our time, energy, and affection; sometimes, we have to say NO to safeguard our YES.

But the little things are different. Too often, we have a knee-jerk NO response to people who get in our way. We don't want to break our stride; our thing is obviously more important than their thing. But here's the thing: the person trying to get our attention is also a person, doing a job or seeking information or needing something that frankly it wouldn't kill us to give. More to the point, that person is a child of God, no less beloved than you or I. Why not increase the goodness in the world by saying YES more often—even if it means taking a lengthy survey about condiments?

When do you default to NO? What story are you telling yourself when you brush off someone in need? Who can you resolve to open yourself to, the next time you have a chance?

CHAPTER 26

Finding God in Pure Gift

Faithful friends are a sturdy shelter; whoever finds one finds a treasure.
—SIRACH 6:14

I T WASN'T A GIVEN THAT WE WOULD BE FRIENDS.

I was an only child until just a few weeks before my eighth-grade graduation. My new brother served to diffuse the laser beam of my parents' attention, which was convenient, but he also required a great deal of babysitting, which was not. I was busy being a teenager, and then moved out for good after college, living in four states over the following eight years. I sent him postcards. He sent me drawings. I visited at holidays. He cried when I left. We were distant enough in age never to fight over the same toy, but we didn't have much to talk about, either.

Eventually, two life-changing things happened: Stephen went to college, and then he came out. Suddenly, we had *so much* to talk about. Not only because he'd finally hit an age I knew how to talk to—I'd been working with college students for years by then—but also because I had a number of close friends who were gay men. Stephen had met them, helping me move from one apartment to the next, and he could see how profoundly I cherished them. In a family whose reaction was wholly unpredictable, I had demonstrated (albeit unknowingly) that I was a safe person to confide in. This brought us close, despite the distance in our ages.

Our friendship wasn't a given, but it has been a godsend. As grownups living a hundred miles apart, Stephen and I talk on the phone almost every day, keeping each other company on our morning walks or drives. We work in similar fields, have overlapping friends (who still can't believe how much we resemble each other), and sing for family weddings and funerals. We share travel adventures, and say the same thing at the same time in the same way with eye-rolling frequency. No one makes me laugh harder. He is my best friend.

Starting when Stephen was in his late twenties, we lost both of our parents to cancer in the course of just seven years. In the end, with Mom gone and Dad on hospice care, we lived back at the homestead for two months, after which we had to sell the house and settle the estate. To say it was a rough patch would be a wicked understatement, yet there we were, together. We took turns being the good kid when the other's last nerve was frayed. We helped each other laugh, and let each other cry. We threw great funerals.

I know that many people endure family tragedy without strong sibling relationships (whether it is the siblings or the relationships that are lacking), but I can't imagine going through those terrible years without my brother. Yet, having spent fourteen years as an only child, I know that not only our friendship, but Stephen's very *existence* was not a given. Maybe that's why I rarely take him for granted. He is, to me, pure gift from God: shocking, unmerited, extraordinary gift. I am grateful beyond measure.

Who (or what) would you describe as pure gift from God in your life? Hold that gratitude in prayer. How do you respond to such a gift? How might you?

CHAPTER 27

Finding God at the Water's Edge

Cast all your worries upon him because he cares for you.
—1 PETER 5:7

I WAS THE FIRST GRANDCHILD ON MY MOTHER'S SIDE OF THE FAMILY, but I was the last *girl* to be born for the next thirty-six years. When the seemingly endless chain of grandsons and great-grandsons was finally broken, I became the godmother of a precious baby named Elizabeth. As soon as she was old enough to talk, she nick-named herself "Bizzy" and set out to win (or at least woo) the world. Not having children of my own, I was unprepared for all the ways this sassy lass would tug at my heart and soul.

My favorite memory of Bizzy is jumping the waves with her in ankle-deep surf at the Jersey shore when she was five years old. I can still see her, dancing impatiently, eager for the next big one. Though she was just a tiny scrap of a thing—near the bottom of the pediatrician's growth chart—she was already fiercely independent. She did not want to be held or touched at all until a "giant" wave loomed over her, at which point she would throw her arms in the air for me to scoop her out of harm's way. Then, screaming with laughter, she'd land, wriggle away, and ready herself again. Her capacity for this adventure was infinite; she would continue until a parent forcibly removed her or I persuaded her to help me build a sandcastle instead (thus rescuing my aching back).

How utterly trusting Bizzy was that day! She never once turned around to make sure I was there. Time and again, faced with a rushing wave as tall as her little self, she simply flung her arms high in the air with perfect confidence that a benevolent universe (in the person of an unflagging godmother) would rescue her.

Though this is not what one is supposed to be thinking about on a beautiful day at the beach, I found myself wondering how long it would be before life shattered that trust. When would something more powerful than a wave come along, that no one who loved her could protect her from? What would be the first deep sorrow of her life? Who would be the first person she trusted unwisely? And how would that affect her?

Looking at her skinny arms thrown confidently in the air, I flung heavenward a prayer for her protection, begging God that she would be able to hold that posture, spiritually, for as long as possible. *May she trust You*, I prayed, *even after life has wounded her and people have let her down. May she never grow guarded or bitter. May the resilience that drives her back into that surf keep her rushing into life with glee and delight, always.*

Come to think of it, I'd really like to maintain that posture myself.

Experiment with a bit of body prayer. Stretch your arms above your head. Reach toward heaven, and imagine yourself entrusting your life to God's care. What are you feeling? Is there anything you want to say to God? Can you sense God's response?

CHAPTER 28

Finding God in a Fortune Cookie

I have set before you life and death, the blessing and the curse.
Choose life, then, that you and your descendants may live . . .
—DEUTERONOMY 30:19

IT WAS LATE IN THE DAY ON A SNOWY SATURDAY IN FEBRUARY, the third weekend in a row I'd spent cleaning out the home of my dear cousin Susan, who had battled a brain tumor for four years before leaving this life at age forty-six. Anyone who has been faced with a similar task knows how wrenching it is. We had to touch and make decisions about literally every object Susan owned, from family heirlooms to frozen hotdogs, from old snapshots to office supplies. It was exhausting. Almost finished with the kitchen, I opened one last drawer and tossed a stash of takeout menus into the recycling bin. Way back in a corner of the drawer was a single fortune cookie, wrapped in its hermetically sealed little bag.

I almost threw it away unopened. But technically, it was Susan's last fortune, and suddenly I was intensely curious about what it said. I opened the wrapper and broke apart the cookie. The tiny slip of paper inside said:

You can't choose how you will die, but you can choose how you will live.

And so she had. Susan didn't choose her brain tumor, but she made amazing choices about how she lived her life—always, but especially in those last four years, right up to her final weeks. Her daughters were just thirteen and sixteen when she got sick, and she willingly endured any treatment that might keep her around for even a bit more of their lives, including three brain surgeries, the lifetime limit of radiation to her head, and daily chemo pills for months at a time. Through all that, she stayed ridiculously optimistic and outrageously funny, keeping us laughing almost as hard as we cried.

About two months before she died, having lost half her vision and most of her words, Susan worked with me to compose a letter to be read at her memorial service, thanking everyone who had been a significant part of her life. Her final line said simply, "I'm so lucky."

Susan was ambivalent about God and completely uninterested in religion, but she had so many of the joyful qualities one would hope to find in a person of faith. She was spirited, loving, passionately on the side of any underdog, and completely unselfconscious. She chose life, always.

I'm not sure most of us know how often that choice lies before us. What attitude am I going to bring into this day? Can I do one thing that is good for my body, my mind, or my spirit? How am I going to treat the person right in front of me? Will I take a risk to pursue a dream?

It is, as they say, a matter of life and death.

Choose wisely!

Think of a dilemma you are facing, whether it's a major decision or simply how you are going to handle a difficult conversation. What is the life-giving choice?

Praying

It doesn't have to be
the blue iris, it could be
weeds in a vacant lot, or a few
small stones; just
pay attention, then patch

a few words together and don't try
to make them elaborate, this isn't
a contest but the doorway

into thanks, and a silence in which
another voice may speak.

—Mary Oliver

Questions for Groups

I WROTE *Finding God in Ordinary Time* with the individual reader in mind, but I can also imagine it as a fruitful resource for faith-sharing groups. If you are praying with this book in the company of others, here are additional questions you might consider together.

Regarding the book as a whole:
- Which of the four "terrains" is most familiar to you? Most foreign?
- In which do you find it easiest / most challenging to spot the presence of God?
- Is there an area in which you feel called to be more attentive? What can you do to cultivate your noticing?

Within any of the terrains:
- Which of the reflections spoke to you the most? Why do you think that is?
- Was there one you found more difficult to connect with? What didn't work for you?
- If your group were writing a series of reflections on this topic, which story from your own life would you contribute?

Origins and Observations:
- How do you feel about your prayer life? What is going well? What makes you anxious or frustrated? What is your deepest desire for your relationship with God?
- What was the starting point in your image of God? Closer to "angry old white guy with a beard," or "alarmingly blank piece of paper?" (Or something else entirely?) How has your image evolved over time, and what helped that to happen?
- Moments of awe may be rare, but they are also real. Can you talk about a time when you were suddenly, unquestionably conscious of the presence/goodness/majesty of God?

Awake to See:

- What was your experience of nature as a child? For good or for ill, how does that affect your ability to find God in the natural world now?
- Where is your favorite place to be outdoors? What is your history there? What shifts inside you when you are in those surroundings?
- Do you feel drawn to spend more time in nature? If so, how can you make that happen?

Messengers of Grace:

- Do you consider yourself an introvert or an extrovert? How does that affect your ability to encounter God in other people?
- Each of us comes from a particular set of demographics. How do yours (age, race, ethnicity, gender, sexual orientation, gender identity, educational background, class, income level, faith tradition, political affiliation, etc.) shape your response to people whose story is different from your own?
- What was the most surprising encounter you ever had with a stranger?

Far From Home:

- What is the farthest you have ever been from home, geographically or culturally? What was that like for you? What did you learn there that you didn't know here?
- Part of the goodness of travel is that it teaches us the relativity of our own culture—the fact that there is more than one valid way to do things. Have you ever experienced such a shift in perspective? Did it stick?
- Is there a place to which you would return in a heartbeat if you had the chance, to visit or even to live? What is it about that place that calls to you? What are you like when you're there?

Working It Out:

- We learn so much more from our failures than we do from our successes. What have your imperfections taught you about God? Yourself? Other people?
- Tragedy often challenges us to think through what we *really* believe about God, at the extremes of distress and sorrow. If there was an incident in your

life that forced you to reexamine your understanding, what happened? Did you affirm an existing belief, or reach a new conclusion?

- What, in your life or in our world, makes you ask, "Where is God in all this?"

Sometimes, it is much easier to talk about what's happening "out there" than to honestly acknowledge the gifts and challenges right in front of us. God has given you to one another for whatever time you have been part of this group. And since *everything* has the potential to call forth a deepening of your life in God (thank you, Saint Ignatius), here are some questions to help wring a few more drops of grace from that sponge.

Finding God Together:

- How have the people in this group helped to call forth a deepening of your life in God?
- Nature is not the only thing with God's fingerprints all over it—so is *human* nature. What qualities of our creator have you noticed in the members of this group?
- When has someone in the group been a messenger of grace for you? What was the message? Were you able to receive it?

- Even members of the same group can sometimes feel foreign to one another. Did anyone come from a very different place, or approach things from a radically different perspective? How did you respond to that new way of seeing?
- Were there times when you were able to let yourself be vulnerable with this group? What risks did you take to share your fears, flaws, or failures? How did others react?
- Where was God in all this?

Scripture Index

The Holy Bible: New Revised Standard Version, 1989.
†*La Biblia Latinoamérica*, edición revisada, 1995.

**La Biblia Latinoamérica,* edición revisada, 1995.

Acknowledgements

MY EARLIEST RECOLLECTION OF PRAYER is a story my mother loved to tell about taking me to a novena (nine days of special prayers in church, often with a particular intention in mind) when I was three years old. Explaining the concept of intercession, Mom posed this question: *Was there something I'd like to ask God for?* I didn't have to dig far to uncover the deepest desire of my heart. Immediately, I replied, "I would like to ask God to make me able to read to myself!" My mother laughed. She loved nothing better than reading to me; it just hadn't occurred to her to start teaching me yet. She took me to church, and then she went to buy flash cards. And so my prayer was answered, not in the magical way I'd hoped, but in the ordinary manner so many prayers are: one human being responding to the need of another. This book is being published on the eleventh anniversary of my mother's death; I chose the date out of gratitude for the many ways Maureen Eberle cultivated my early love of both God and words.

A first book warrants a lifetime of acknowledgements. Special thanks, therefore, go to:

- My father, William Eberle, who also loved to read, and my whole extended family: aunts, uncles, and cousins. (Special shout-out to my goddaughter Elizabeth DeStefano, the "sassy lass" of the first essay I wrote for this collection, who turns seventeen on the book's publication date.)

- My dear cousin Susan Eberle, who thought I could do anything. Miss you every day, darlin'.

- The two religious sisters who were my best writing coaches: my fifth-grade teacher, Sr. Marian Counsuela, RSM (now Sr. Marian Robinson) and my twelfth-grade English teacher, Sr. Dolores Kathryn, IHM (now Sr. Rosemary Davis). I can honestly say I remember all of my vocabulary words, and most of my affirmations.

- The two Jesuit priests who introduced me to Ignatian spirituality in college: Fr. Pat Earl, who taught the course *Jesuit Spirit in Action*, and Fr. Rob McChesney, who directed my first silent retreat and showed me a whole new way of experiencing God.

- Susan Bowers Baker, my long-time spiritual director, whose tender and fiery regard is a source of deep consolation.
- Fr. Sam Verruni, my colleague for ten years at West Chester University's Newman Center, whose collaborative approach to preaching honed my impromptu sermon-crafting skills.
- My friend Ron Knapp, who insisted that I had a book in me, and challenged me to articulate the concept that became *Finding God in Ordinary Time*.
- My fellow writers and the staff at When Words Count Retreat—especially Steve Eisner—for believing that this book belonged out in the wider world, as well as Dede Cummings and the staff at Green Writers Press, for taking a chance on what I thought of as "my little God book."
- The colorful characters / dear friends in my St. Vincent's and Campus Ministry faith-sharing groups, who keep me both grounded and searching.
- My Gwynedd Mercy University community: everyone who listened to chapter drafts and made helpful suggestions; my colleagues who stretched to cover the absences this writing process entailed; and especially S. Kati McMahon, RSM, who has mentored my personal and professional development in merciful ways for fourteen years and counting.

- Peggy Moran, my original editor, whose tireless, insightful, and humorous approach to her job transformed the potentially tedious work of editing into a near-constant joy. It is because of you that I know why so many authors thank their editors.
- My dear friends Mary Ellen Graham and Ann-Therese Ortiz, who accepted the challenge of reading the early manuscript and suggesting which chapters to omit in order to get us to twenty-eight. I do not hold it against either of you.
- Lauren Humphries Dangelmeier, my very own grammar girl, who always responded to frantic texts about word usage and the nuances of commas.
- My brother, Stephen Eberle, with whom I have clarified my thoughts by perseverating on topics both profound and ridiculous as we've taken our morning walks in separate cities for the past many years. You know and love me in equal measure, as I do you.
- My sweetheart, Porter Bush, who never once said, "Aren't you done yet?" You have held my hand through so many losses. I am grateful to be imagining our way together into the future, whatever it holds.

To all who see themselves somewhere in these pages: thank you. Because of you, my ordinary days have been extraordinarily blessed.